I Am
Roberto Clemente

By Jim Gigliotti

Illustrated by
Ute Simon

SCHOLASTIC INC.

No part of this publication may be reproduced, stored in a retrieval system, or transmitted in any form or by any means, electronic, mechanical, photocopying, recording, or otherwise, without written permission of the publisher. For information regarding permission, write to Scholastic Inc., Attention: Permissions Department, 557 Broadway, New York, NY 10012.

ISBN 978-0-545-53381-2

10 9 8 7 6 5 4   13 14 15 16 17 18/0

Printed in the U.S.A.   40
First printing, August 2013

Cover illustration by Mark Fredrickson
Interior illustrations by Ute Simon

Contents

Introduction

If you ever saw me as I was growing up in Puerto Rico, I probably had a baseball in my hands. Either I was playing baseball with my friends or I was throwing a baseball against the wall outside my family's house in Carolina, Puerto Rico, and catching it. And if I wasn't playing baseball, then I was probably watching my favorite players in the Puerto Rican Winter League. As far back as I can remember, I wanted to be a baseball player, just like them.

When I was born, black players were not allowed to play Major League Baseball—what is called the "big leagues"—in the United States. But in 1947, when I was a teenager, Jackie Robinson became the first black man to play in the big leagues in the twentieth century. That made it possible for black players like me to follow.

In fact, while I was black like Jackie Robinson, I also was a black Latin American. (Jackie was not Latin American. He was born in the United States.) There were very few black Latinos playing when I made it to Major League Baseball. We spoke Spanish, and sometimes it was hard for us to communicate. We were treated poorly, a lot like black American players were when they first began playing in the big leagues.

Where I grew up in Puerto Rico, there were no rules that black people couldn't eat at the same places or stay at the same places as white people. But when I got to the United States, there were such rules in some cities. I couldn't believe it! And I certainly didn't like it. I believed that all people, not just Latinos, deserved to be treated properly.

I made it to the big leagues in 1955. Over my eighteen-year career, I became one of the greatest right fielders in Major League Baseball history. I could hit for average, hit for power, and run, field, and throw the ball well. I was what big-league scouts call "a five-tool player." Five-tool players are rare.

I believed that my athletic ability was a gift from God. I also believed if God gave me that gift when other people didn't have anything, then I should reach out to help them. While I grew up in Puerto Rico, my family wasn't poor, but we didn't have extra money, either. I always tried to help people who didn't have everything they needed.

Mostly, though, I was an inspiration to Latin American baseball players around the world. Some great Latino ballplayers that followed me say that I was their Jackie Robinson. I was not the first Latin American player in the big leagues. But most people say I was the first Latino to become a superstar. And I was the first Latino player to be inducted into the National Baseball Hall of Fame. I am Roberto Clemente.

ROBERTO CLEMENTE WALKER
PITTSBURGH N. L. 1955-1972

MEMBER OF EXCLUSIVE 3,000-HIT CLUB. LED
NATIONAL LEAGUE IN BATTING FOUR TIMES. HAD
FOUR SEASONS WITH 200 OR MORE HITS WHILE
POSTING LIFETIME .317 AVERAGE AND 240 HOME
RUNS. WON MOST VALUABLE PLAYER AWARD 1966.
RIFLE-ARMED DEFENSIVE STAR SET N. L. MARK BY
PACING OUTFIELDERS IN ASSISTS FIVE YEARS.
BATTED .362 IN TWO WORLD SERIES, HITTING IN
ALL 14 GAMES.

9

People You Will Meet

ROBERTO CLEMENTE:
Hall of Fame baseball player for the Pittsburgh Pirates from 1955 to 1972. He was also one of the game's greatest humanitarians and an inspirational figure for Latin Americans.

MONTE IRVIN:
A great baseball player when Roberto was growing up. The two became friends, and Monte became a role model for Roberto.

LUISA CLEMENTE:
Roberto's mother. Roberto was the youngest of her seven children. She dreamed that he would grow up to be an engineer.

MELCHOR CLEMENTE:
Roberto's father. He was a foreman in the sugarcane fields in Puerto Rico.

PEDRÍN ZORILLA:
The owner of the Santurce Cangrejeros, a team in the Puerto Rican Winter League. In 1952, he signed Roberto to his first professional baseball contract.

ROBERTO MARÍN:[*]
A rice salesman who managed a local team in Carolina, Puerto Rico. He asked Roberto to join the team after seeing the fourteen–year–old playing in a neighborhood game.

AL CAMPANIS:
A scout for Major League Baseball's Brooklyn Dodgers. He filed a glowing report on Roberto in the early 1950s. In 1954, the Dodgers asked Roberto to play for their team.

HOWIE HAAK:
A scout for Major League Baseball's Pittsburgh Pirates. When Roberto thought about quitting in 1954, Howie convinced him to keep playing.

VERA ZABALA:
Roberto's wife. She also was from Carolina, Puerto Rico. When she and Roberto got married in 1964, it was cause for great celebration in their hometown.

Time Line

August 18, 1934

Roberto Clemente is born in Carolina, Puerto Rico.

1952

Roberto plays professional baseball for the first time when he joins the Santurce Cangrejeros team of the Puerto Rican Winter League.

April 17, 1955

At twenty years old, Roberto plays in the big leagues for the first time, with the Pirates.

July 25, 1956

Roberto hits an inside-the-park grand slam to beat the Chicago Cubs in the bottom of the ninth inning.

1961

Roberto wins the first of twelve consecutive Gold Glove Awards for his play in right field.

November 14, 1964

Roberto marries Vera Zabala in Carolina, Puerto Rico.

September 30, 1972

Roberto gets his 3,000th career hit against the New York Mets' Jon Matlack in the fourth inning of the Pirates' 5–0 victory.

October 3, 1972

Roberto comes off the bench to play in right field against St. Louis for his final appearance in a regular-season game.

February 19, 1954

Roberto signs a contract with Major League Baseball's Brooklyn Dodgers organization and he joins the club's minor-league team in Montreal.

November 22, 1954

Roberto is drafted away from the Dodgers by the Pittsburgh Pirates.

July 11, 1960

Roberto plays for the National League in the All-Star Game for the first time.

1960

Roberto has at least one hit in every game to help Pittsburgh win a thrilling seven-game World Series over the New York Yankees.

1966

Roberto earns the National League's Most Valuable Player award.

July 24, 1970

Roberto is honored at Three Rivers Stadium in Pittsburgh on Roberto Clemente Night.

1971

Roberto is named the Most Valuable Player of the Pirates' World Series victory over the Baltimore Orioles.

December 31, 1972

Roberto is killed in a plane crash near San Juan, Puerto Rico, while traveling to deliver supplies to earthquake victims in Nicaragua. He is just thirty-eight years old.

August 6, 1973

Roberto is **posthumously** inducted into the National Baseball Hall of Fame.

CHAPTER ONE

A Passion for *Béisbol*

"Roberto!" his mother would call from inside the family's house in San Antón, a **barrio** in the small town of Carolina, Puerto Rico. "Time to come in for dinner!"

Almost every time, Roberto's response was the same. "One moment! One moment!" he'd yell. Sometimes it was just, "Moment! Moment!" Or, in Spanish, *"Momentito!"*

Roberto said *"Momentito!"* so many times that his family shortened it and simply called out "Momen!" when someone needed him. The nickname stuck. The family called Roberto "Momen" for the rest of his life.

More often than not, Momen didn't want to come in when he was called because he was outside playing baseball until the sun went down. "I would forget to eat because of baseball," he said later in his life.

Baseball—or *béisbol* in Spanish—was the most popular sport for kids in Puerto Rico when Roberto was growing up. Of course, there also was soccer, which is popular everywhere in the world. Roberto participated in track and field, too, where his speed made him a good sprinter and where his incredible right arm allowed him to excel in the javelin. The javelin is a spear about eight feet two inches long that is thrown by hand. Roberto once set his high school record for the javelin throw. But it was baseball that was Roberto's passion. He and his neighborhood friends in Carolina would be happy to play baseball all day and into the night.

Baseball has been played in Puerto Rico since the late 1800s. Americans and Cubans brought the game to the island, which is located in the Caribbean Sea, between the Dominican Republic and the Virgin Islands. Puerto Rico is about a two-and-a-half-hour flight from Miami, Florida.

Puerto Rico became an American territory after the Spanish-American War, which ended in 1898. Before that, the island belonged to Spain. Christopher Columbus claimed it for Spain when he landed there in 1493. In 1508, the famous explorer Juan Ponce de León arrived. He eventually established a settlement he called Puerto Rico (meaning "Rich Port"). That port is now San Juan, the capital city.

Today, Puerto Rico remains an American territory—it belongs to the United States of America but has not been granted statehood—and its citizens are U.S. citizens. But the Puerto Ricans' primary language is Spanish.

Carolina is a city in the northern part of Puerto Rico. It is about twelve miles southeast of San Juan, which is at the island's northern tip. In 1935, shortly after Roberto was born,

Carolina had about 21,000 residents, according to the U.S. Census. It has since grown to more than 176,000 residents.

Today, Puerto Rico is a popular tourist destination, especially for people from the continental United States. Visitors marvel at the beauty of its beaches and its natural landscape. They go on vacation for adventures such as

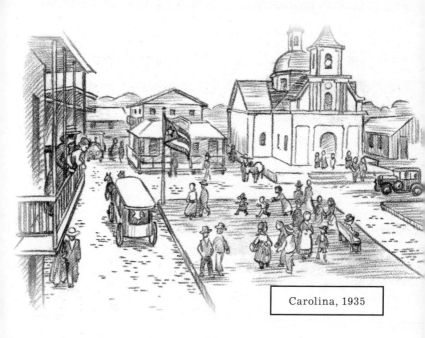

Carolina, 1935

snorkeling or scuba diving, or to explore the cultural history of the island.

When Roberto was growing up, though, Puerto Rico was mostly made of **rural** communities. Many of the men in Carolina worked in the sugarcane fields. They spent long, hot days in the sun chopping down sugarcane with their **machetes**.

Momen was born in Carolina to one of those sugarcane workers. Momen's given name was Roberto Clemente Walker, and he was born on August 18, 1934. In many Hispanic cultures, a child's full legal name includes both the family name (in Roberto's case, Clemente, from his dad's side) and the mom's maiden name (Walker).

Roberto's father, Melchor, was a foreman in the sugarcane fields. His mother, Luisa, would get up in the early hours of the morning to make lunches for Melchor and for the other men in the fields. The men had to be at work as soon

as it was light enough so they could get going
before the sun was too strong.

Luisa had a boy, Luis, and a girl, Rosa, from
an earlier marriage. After her first husband
died, Luisa married Melchor. Together, Melchor
and Luisa had five children, including four

boys: Osvaldo, Justino, Andres, and Roberto. Their daughter, Anairis, was only five years old when she died in a fire. Roberto was their youngest child.

Family was important to Roberto. Even though the Clementes didn't have a lot of money, Roberto happily remembered the nights spent together at home. The family would eat and talk and joke with one another. "It was something wonderful to me," he said.

Roberto went to school. He had plenty of friends. Sometimes he helped his father in the sugarcane fields. But mostly he liked to play baseball. When he wasn't playing baseball, he still carried around a ball. He'd toss it against the wall or throw it in the air and catch it.

The ball wasn't always a real ball, though. Roberto was born in the 1930s. That was the middle of the Great Depression in the United States, and times were tough in many places around the world. The Clemente family was one of the lucky ones. Melchor had a decent job, and he was able to provide the necessities for his family.

Baseball equipment was another story, though. That was a luxury. So Roberto did what lots of others kids did. Some rolled-up rags worked almost as well as a real baseball. An old broomstick worked almost as well as a real baseball bat. Sometimes, a branch from a **guava** tree would do for a bat. And an old, smashed tin can would do for a ball. Imagine how good a hitter Roberto had to be to smack a tin can with a broomstick!

It didn't bother him to play with **makeshift** equipment. Roberto was just glad to have food on the table and clothes on his back. "I grew up with people who really had to struggle to eat," he said.

That's a big reason Roberto never turned his back on people in need, even after he became a star baseball player in the United States. It's also a big reason Roberto learned early in his life to appreciate the value of money and hard work.

It's easy to imagine Roberto riding his bicycle around Carolina to meet his friends to play *béisbol*. One time, they played a game that lasted all day long, and Roberto hit ten home runs.

Baseball During the Great Depression

Money was scarce during the Great Depression, but baseball survived. Fans remained loyal to their teams, though they didn't have a lot of money to go to the games. Major League attendance, which had set records in the late 1920s, dropped sharply.

Some good came out of that, though. Big–league teams had to be creative to drum up interest. So teams began broadcasting their games live on the radio. To get folks to the ballpark, they started promotions such as Ladies' Day. And the biggest  **innovation** was that teams began playing games at night. The first big–league game under the lights was in 1935, when the Cincinnati Reds hosted the Philadelphia Phillies at Crosley Field.

Another time, when Roberto was fourteen years old, a man named Roberto Marín couldn't help but notice how far Roberto could hit the ball and how fast he could run. He asked Roberto to play for a team he managed. It wasn't exactly baseball. It was softball, which is played with a larger ball (which is not that soft!) on a smaller field. And it was for a local team sponsored by the Sello Rojo rice-packaging company, not a professional team. Still, Roberto was happy to play. It was the first time he ever played in an organized league.

Big-League Dreams

Young Roberto climbed a tree outside Sixto Escobar Stadium in San Juan, Puerto Rico. The stadium was named after a world-champion boxer, but Roberto was there for baseball. His favorite team, the San Juan Senadores (which means "Senators"), was playing the rival Santurce Cangrejeros (which means "Crabbers").

Roberto liked to watch the professional players in Puerto Rico and dream of one day becoming like them. The Senadores played in the Puerto Rican Winter League. In the winter months, when it was cold across most of the United States but the weather was still warm in the Caribbean, professional players from Major League Baseball and from the Negro Leagues would **migrate** to Puerto Rico. Free from the cold weather, they could continue to play baseball to stay sharp and get ready for spring training.

It cost Roberto ten cents to take the bus to the ballpark, so he didn't always have the extra fifteen cents to get inside the stadium. Climbing a tree to peek inside, then, was the next-best thing. True, he couldn't see the players up close like he could from the inside, but the view of the outfield wasn't bad. And that's where his favorite player, the Senadores' Monte Irvin, played.

Monte was a star for the Newark Eagles in the Negro National League. He started playing winter baseball in Puerto Rico in the 1940s, when Roberto was still a boy, and he soon made an impression on Momen. Sometimes, before Roberto would take his spot in the tree, he would stand outside the players' entrance to the stadium to get a glimpse of Monte and some of his teammates as they walked by.

One day, Monte noticed Roberto and began talking to him. "Will you carry my bag for me?" Monte asked. Of course he would! Roberto was thrilled to help out his idol. Monte didn't really need someone to carry his equipment bag, but it was his way of getting Roberto into the game for free.

That began a long friendship. Many times, Monte handed his bag to Roberto and asked the boy to carry it for him. When he was a teenager, Roberto dreamed of someday becoming a star like Monte. Roberto's mom also dreamed that one day her son would grow up to be successful—but not as a baseball player. She wanted him

to become an engineer. Sometimes, she thought he spent too much time playing baseball. And when he got in trouble one day, she started to burn his bat as a punishment. "I got it out of the fire and saved it," Roberto said.

It was a good thing Roberto was able to save his bat, because his ability to swing that bat was getting him noticed. When Roberto was sixteen years old, he joined an amateur baseball team called the Juncos Mules. While playing for the Mules, he caught the attention of Pedrín Zorilla.

Pedrín was the owner of the Santurce Cangrejeros in the Puerto Rican Winter League. He fell in love with baseball on a trip to the

United States during the 1910s. Pedrín went on to become one of the most important figures in the history of baseball in Puerto Rico. A friend of Pedrín's suggested that Pedrín watch Roberto play. In 1952, Pedrín saw Roberto play in a Juncos game. He soon signed Roberto to his first professional contract. At eighteen years old, Roberto was making forty dollars a week to play the game he loved.

Pedrín, meanwhile, was making friends in Major League Baseball. One of these was Brooklyn Dodgers scout Al Campanis. A former player, Al first visited Puerto Rico in 1950, when he organized a baseball camp in the city of Aguadilla. "They're baseball crazy down there," he marveled to a reporter on his return to the mainland United States.

Al soon became a respected figure in the Caribbean. He spoke Spanish and developed a **rapport** with the Latin American players, several of whom he signed to contracts with the Dodgers. One of them, Cuba's Sandy Amoros, starred for Brooklyn in the 1955 World Series.

Not long after Roberto signed with Santurce, Pedrín arranged for Al to host a tryout at Sixto Escobar Stadium. The tryout was an open audition for a professional contract. Seventy-two players showed up, but it was only Roberto who caught Al's eye. In fact, even before Roberto hit, he wowed Al with his throwing arm and speed.

Roberto was still in high school at the time, though, so a Major League contract would have to wait. In the meantime, he spent the 1952 season mostly sitting on the bench for Santurce.

He didn't play much because the Cangrejeros already had several stars, and the club wanted him to learn from the older players on the team. By his second season, though, Roberto was ready. He had sixty-three hits in sixty games and played great defense.

In 1954, the Dodgers signed Roberto to a contract: a $10,000 bonus, plus a $5,000 salary. At nineteen years old, he would begin his career in the minor leagues. The minor leagues are the different levels of pro baseball in which potential Major League Baseball players get training and experience. Most minor-league teams have a specific Major League team with which they work. The Dodgers' top minor-league team at the time was the Montreal Royals of the International League. Roberto was on his way to Canada to join the Royals.

The Negro Leagues

Until 1947, Major League Baseball had an unofficial "color barrier." Though no official rule existed, black players were not welcome. They played in their own leagues, called the Negro Leagues.

The Negro Leagues included several different leagues, with the most famous being the Negro National League. The original Negro National League began in 1920 when Andrew "Rube" Foster organized black baseball clubs in the Midwest. That earned Foster distinction as the "Father of Black Baseball."

In the mid–1930s, the most famous Negro Leagues team was the Pittsburgh Crawfords. The Crawfords featured legendary pitcher Leroy "Satchel" Paige. He eventually pitched in the Major Leagues until he was forty–seven years old—not counting one game for the Kansas City Athletics in 1965 when he was fifty–nine!

The Crawfords' lineup also included catcher Josh Gibson. He was such a great hitter that he was sometimes called the "black Babe Ruth." Speedy outfielder James "Cool Papa" Bell was perhaps the fastest man ever to play pro baseball.

Infielder Jackie Robinson, who played for the Negro Leagues' Kansas City Monarchs in 1945, broke the Major League color barrier when he joined the Brooklyn Dodgers in 1947. As more and more black players joined Major League Baseball, the Negro Leagues eventually dissolved. The last of the Negro Leagues played in the early 1960s. The leagues are still remembered today at the Negro Leagues Baseball Museum in Kansas City, Missouri.

CHAPTER THREE

Culture Shock

Roberto got off the plane in Montreal and entered a whole new world. One teammate later said that it was "a cultural twilight zone for him."

Montreal is in the province of Quebec, which is divided between English- and French-speaking residents. Roberto spoke only a little English, and no French.

And then there was the weather. In the six months of the baseball season (from April

through September), the average temperature in Montreal is about sixty-nine degrees. That was a huge change for a man who was used to the heat of San Juan, where the average temperature is almost ninety degrees during the summer.

Roberto didn't socialize with his teammates much because it was hard to talk with them. He did become friends with shortstop Chico Fernández, who was from Cuba. But when Roberto first got to Montreal, Chico was the only other player from the Caribbean. Roberto and Chico sometimes hung out with Joe Black. He was an African American pitcher who already had played a few seasons with the Brooklyn Dodgers and was trying to make it back to the Major Leagues. Joe could tell Roberto and Chico about life in the big leagues—and he could speak some Spanish, too.

A white American player named Tommy Lasorda also spoke some Spanish. Tommy was a pitcher for the Royals. He later would become famous as the long-time manager of the Los Angeles Dodgers in the 1970s, 1980s, and 1990s. Tommy and Roberto would go out to restaurants, and Tommy would help Roberto with the English on the menus.

That was when they went out in Montreal, or in cities such as Toronto, Canada, and Buffalo, New York. In 1954, though, Roberto sometimes had to travel to play games in the southern United States, where Jim Crow laws—legal **segregation** of public places—still existed. When Roberto traveled to Richmond, Virginia, to play a game against the Richmond Virginians, he encountered segregation for the first time. He didn't understand it. In Puerto Rico, Canada, and New York, white and black players ate at the same restaurants and played on the same fields. In Montreal, he and Chico lived with a white family in their home. In Richmond,

though, they couldn't stay in a hotel with their white teammates, and they couldn't eat at the same places.

Just as hard to understand was why he wasn't playing much baseball. Roberto was confused and frustrated because he had played little for the Royals and spent most of his time on the bench.

Once, he was pulled out of the game with the bases loaded, and a pinch hitter was called in to bat for him. And it was only the first inning! Another time, the coaches kept Roberto on the sidelines even though he had hit three triples the day before. In a six-game series in Havana against the Cuban team in the International League, Roberto didn't play a single game.

Roberto didn't understand why he wasn't spending more time on the field, playing the sport he loved. When the Dodgers drafted him, they had paid him a big bonus. But the Royals

didn't seem to want Roberto. Roberto didn't understand—was he not playing well enough? What was going on?

Roberto was so frustrated that he decided he would give up. He packed his bags and got ready to go to the airport. He would go back to Puerto Rico before the season was over. His big-league dreams would be dashed.

Fortunately, a Pittsburgh Pirates' scout caught up with Roberto before he could leave for the airport. The scout's name was Howie Haak (pronounced "Hake"). Howie explained what had been happening. It wasn't that Roberto wasn't playing well enough for the Royals—it was the opposite. He was too good!

Howie explained that the Dodgers knew Roberto could be a great player one day. But they already had several excellent outfielders at the big-league level in Brooklyn. So they hoped that if Roberto didn't play a lot, other teams might not notice how talented he was. If another team did notice, they might pick Roberto to play for their team instead during the special draft of minor-league players—the "Rule 5" draft—held at the end of the season.

But Howie and the Pittsburgh Pirates had already noticed Roberto. Howie told Roberto the Pirates planned to choose Roberto in the special draft. Roberto would be playing in the big leagues the next season. He just had to be patient.

So Roberto went back to the Royals. He would finish out the season with them and wait for the Pirates to draft him. Roberto made the best of the rest of the season. He had three hits in one game against Syracuse. And he had three more hits in a shutout of Richmond. Then, during one game in August, Roberto sealed the Royals' 8–7 victory over Toronto. He threw out the potential tying runner at the plate from

right field to end the game.

After the season, Howie made good on his promise. The Pirates selected Roberto in the Rule 5 draft. Roberto would make his big-league **debut** in Pittsburgh in 1955. He couldn't wait.

Late in 1954, Roberto did get back on the field with Santurce in the Puerto Rican Winter League. All winter long, he looked forward to making it to the big leagues in 1955.

To the Big Leagues

In March 1955, Roberto went to his first spring training with the Pittsburgh Pirates. Spring training is when big-league teams work out and get ready for the season by playing games that don't count in the regular standings. In the mid-1950s, the Pirates, like most Major League Baseball teams, held spring training in Florida.

Roberto was excited to join the Pirates, but he didn't like everything about spring training. Just as in Virginia the year before, Roberto encountered Jim Crow laws in Florida. When he got to Fort Myers, where the Pittsburgh team trained, he found that he couldn't stay in the downtown hotel where most of the Pirates stayed. He and a few other dark-skinned teammates had to stay at another hotel, across town. They couldn't eat at the same restaurants as the white players, either.

This was an **injustice**. And any injustice bothered Roberto. He was surprised, saddened— and angry—when he was in Florida.

Sometimes white players would go into a restaurant while the black players had to wait on the bus. The white players would ask the black players if they wanted anything to eat. But one time, Roberto had enough of such treatment. He told one of the other players on the bus that he would never accept anything from a restaurant that treated people that way— and that if the other players did, he would get

into a fight over it with them because Roberto felt it was so unfair.

Still, Roberto didn't let that affect his play on the field. His batting average that spring was almost .400. A batting average is the number of hits a player gets, divided by the number of times the player is at bat. So three hits in every ten at-bats equals a batting average of .300. A batting average of .300 or better is considered excellent, so Roberto's .400 that spring was superb. Roberto showed his manager and teammates what a terrific throwing arm he had, and how great a player he could be one day.

That was good news for the Pirates. They were happy to have Roberto on their team. The Pirates had finished in last place for the third season in a row in 1954, and they were probably going to finish last again in 1955—with or without Roberto! But they could tell he had the potential to develop into an excellent player. When Roberto headed back to Pittsburgh after spring training, he was ready for his first big-league season.

Outside of spring training, Roberto faced the most **discrimination** not from fans or other players, but from the media. Reporters weren't quite sure what to make of Roberto's highly accented English or the **unique** way he had of doing things. For example, he had a habit of stretching and rolling his shoulders before each at-bat. Some members of the press made fun of the way Roberto spoke. In the newspapers, they seemed to enjoy making him sound unintelligent—which was far from the truth, of course. "I heet ball good," they might write. Or, "I theenk I have chance to make home."

And, at first, other Pirates' players weren't quite sure how to approach their new teammate, either. Roberto spoke a language most of them did not. He was quiet off the field and all business on the field. But one teammate Roberto quickly made friends with in 1955

was another **rookie**, Roman Mejias. Roman was another outfielder. He was from Cuba. Roberto and Roman briefly shared a place to live before Roberto moved in with a family that had an extra room to rent in Pittsburgh.

The family, an older African American man and woman with no children, gave Roberto a little sense of home in a town that was very different for him. There wasn't a large black

population in Pittsburgh at the time, and there were even fewer Spanish-speaking citizens.

But while the media and teammates weren't quite sure what to make of Roberto, there was no such uncertainty with the fans. They quickly embraced Roberto's style. They liked the way he played hard every day and zipped from first base to third base on a single to the outfield. And they liked the way he made spectacular catches that turned potential doubles and triples for opposing batters into outs. He was a bright spot in a string of dismal seasons for the Pirates.

In one game in 1956, Roberto came up to bat against the Chicago Cubs in a home game. The Pirates trailed 8–5, with two outs in the bottom of the ninth inning, but they had the bases loaded.

Roberto smashed a ball down the left-field line. It clanged off the foul pole, but was below the top of the wall. Fair ball! The ball rolled along the warning track toward center field, away from the left fielder. One run scored. Two runs scored. Three runs scored. And then there came Roberto, racing around third and heading for home.

Pirates manager Bobby Bragan, who also was the third-base coach, threw his hands in the air. "Stop! Stop!" Bobby yelled to Roberto. Head down, though, Roberto kept barreling for home. Roberto and the throw to the catcher arrived at the plate at just about the same time. Roberto slid . . . safe! The Pirates won,

9–8. It was the first—and still only—walk-off inside-the-park grand slam in Major League history. (A walk-off hit is a hit that ends the game. It's called that because the players "walk off" the field.)

In another game that same year, Roberto raced all the way home to score from first base on a single that barely reached the outfield grass in right field. That was the kind of excitement Roberto brought to the team. Still, the team continued to struggle, finishing in last place in 1955 and next-to-last in 1956 and 1957. Then, in the summer of 1957, Danny Murtaugh became the manager. He had seen Roberto during his rookie season and thought Roberto was destined to be one of the greatest players of all time.

Roberto was not only talented, but he also was pretty smart. After making it to the Major Leagues, he took one look at how large the Pirates' home park, Forbes Field, was. He knew he wouldn't hit a lot of home runs there. So he concentrated on hitting line drives instead. Still, he managed to hit 240 home runs in his career. Only 83 of them, however, came at Forbes Field.

The wide expanses of the Pirates' home field did allow Roberto to show off his great right arm. Early in his career, Roberto threw out pitcher Harvey Haddix at home plate from the outfield. Roberto was more than 400 feet away when he made the throw. Runners soon learned not to test his arm.

As good as he was in the field, though, it was hitting that earned Roberto a spot in his first All-Star Game. It came in 1960. Though he was in his sixth big-league season, he still was only twenty-five years old on Opening Day that year. Roberto broke out that season to post the best regular-season totals of his career so far: a .314 batting average, sixteen home runs, and ninety-four runs batted in. (A player is credited with a run batted in, or "RBI," when what he does at bat results in a run scored for his team.)

More important, the Pirates were finally winning. After many years near the bottom of the National League standings, Pittsburgh finished in second place in 1958. In 1959, the Pirates were fourth. And in 1960, they put it all together to finish first in the league.

Then, the Pirates beat the mighty New York Yankees four games to three in the World Series.

It was a huge upset. In the final game, Pirates second baseman Bill Mazeroski hit one of the most famous home runs in baseball history. It came in the bottom of the ninth inning of the last game to win the Series.

Bill's blast set off a wild celebration. It was the Pirates' first World Series victory since 1925. Roberto played a large role in the victory, getting at least one hit in every game and batting .310.

CHAPTER FIVE

The Pride of Pittsburgh

Roberto's biggest thrill about the 1960 season, he once said, wasn't winning the World Series. It was walking out of the clubhouse after the last game and seeing thousands of fans celebrating in the streets. It was a feeling he later said that he could not describe. He didn't feel like a player among them. He felt like one of the fans. He walked the streets with them, talking with them and celebrating the team's big win.

From the very beginning, it had been a love

affair between Roberto and the Pirates' fans. Sure, at first they may have found it different that he was a Spanish-speaking black man. But he was always polite and talkative with the fans, and he signed every requested autograph after every game.

Not every player did that, of course. Some of the other players were married and wanted to get home to their families. For much of his career, Roberto didn't have a family in

Pittsburgh. Some of the other players wanted to go out and party at night. But Roberto wasn't that type, either. Besides, he remembered what it was like when he was a youngster. He used to wait at the ballpark trying to catch a glimpse of his heroes. Now, he was one of the heroes.

One time, a foul ball was hit into the right-field stands at Pittsburgh's Forbes Field. A young boy reached for it, but an adult man grabbed it away. Roberto noticed the boy crying. The next inning, when Roberto went to his place in the field, he brought out a new ball for the youngster. "Here's a ball for the one they took away from you," Roberto said.

The fans loved him for such kindnesses. And when Roberto came to bat, the fans loved the way he hit. Roberto was the National League's best hitter in the 1960s by quite a bit. He batted an average of .328 for the nine years from 1960 to 1969. The next-best player in the league in

that time span had a .312 batting average. And though not known strictly as a power hitter, Roberto's 177 home runs in that decade were bettered by only ten other players. His 862 RBIs ranked sixth.

"The big thing about Clemente is that he can hit any pitch," San Francisco Giants ace Juan Marichal once said. "I don't mean only strikes. He can hit a ball off his ankles or off his ear." The only way to pitch to him so that he wouldn't be able to get a hit? "Roll the ball," the Dodgers' Sandy Koufax famously once said.

In 1961, the season after the Pirates won the World Series, Roberto had a .351 batting average. It was the best average in the National League that season. He had the league's best average three more times in a four-season span beginning in 1964. In 1966, he hit a career-best twenty-nine home runs and was voted the Most Valuable Player in the National League.

Roberto made the National League All-Star team every year but one during the 1960s. The lone exception was in 1968, when injuries kept him out of thirty games. Even still, he earned a Gold Glove that year for his play in right field for the eighth consecutive year. Eventually, Roberto would win a Gold Glove twelve seasons in a row.

Meanwhile, big things were happening for Roberto off the field, too.

In January 1964, Roberto met Vera Zabala when he was back home in Puerto Rico. Vera was a secretary at the government bank in San Juan. She was also from Carolina. She was smart, beautiful, and shared Roberto's passion for helping others. Roberto noticed her walking to the local pharmacy one day. Vera went into the pharmacy. So did Roberto. They struck up a conversation.

At first, Vera wouldn't go out with Roberto. Vera's father was strict and didn't want her dating anyone. Eventually, though, Vera accepted an invitation to watch Roberto play a game in San Juan. Then Roberto came by her office to take her on a lunch date. It wasn't long before they were engaged to be married.

Less than one year after they met, Roberto and Vera were married in November 1964. It was practically a holiday in Carolina. Roberto Jr. was born on August 17, 1965. Then came

Luis, one year later. A third son, Enrique, was born in 1970.

Also in 1970, the Pirates moved into a new home: Three Rivers Stadium. They had played in Forbes Field for more than sixty years. On July 24, 1970, the Pirates held Roberto Clemente Night at Three Rivers Stadium. The Pirates wanted to honor him for his great play over the years.

Vera and the boys, of course, were there on Roberto Clemente Night. So were Roberto's parents, Melchor and Luisa. Melchor was eighty-seven years old and had never been on an airplane before. But he wasn't about to miss his son's big day.

From the microphone that was set up near home plate that night, Roberto looked up and saw the Three Rivers Stadium stands packed with fans.

He looked toward right field and saw hundreds of spectators in *pavas*, the white straw hats worn by the sugarcane workers in the fields in Puerto Rico.

He looked behind him and saw Melchor and Luisa, Vera, and the boys.

He started to speak . . . and he couldn't. He was overcome with emotion.

He was overwhelmed by the crowd that was about three times the usual size for a Pirates' home game. Overwhelmed by the several planeloads of Puerto Ricans who flew in

because they would not be content with just watching the honor on television or listening on the radio in their native land. Overwhelmed by the presence of family, which was always so important to him.

Roberto composed himself enough to speak. The night was a "triumph for us, the Latinos," he said. "I believe it is a matter of pride for all of us, the Puerto Ricans as well as for all of those in the Caribbean, because we are all brothers."

The team presented Roberto with plenty of gifts, plaques, and trophies. The fans chipped in to make a donation to the Pittsburgh Children's Hospital on behalf of Roberto. And the Pirates' owners announced a special trust fund to pay for the college education of Roberto's sons.

Then Pittsburgh went out and beat the visiting Houston Astros 11–0. As if to thank the fans one more time, Roberto had two singles and made a pair of great catches in the game.

Gold Glove Award

Since 1957, Gold Gloves have been awarded each year by baseball glove—maker Rawlings to the best fielders in the National League and the American League. For each league, one Gold Glove is awarded for pitcher, catcher, first baseman, second baseman, shortstop, and third baseman. Three Gold Gloves are awarded to outfielders, without regard as to whether the player is a right fielder, left fielder, or center fielder.

Roberto's twelve career Gold Gloves are the most for any right fielder, ever. Among all outfielders, only all—time great Willie Mays, who played center field, also has twelve Gold Gloves.

CHAPTER SIX

Making a Difference

Roberto was in his sixteenth big-league season in 1970. The number of Latino players in baseball was growing, and they all admired the man who was the first great Latino player.

The Giants' Juan Marichal was Roberto's friend. So was the Braves' Orlando Cepeda. And the Phillies' Octavio "Cookie" Rojas. And the Alou brothers: Felipe, Jesus, and Matty. And teammates such as Jose Pagan and Manny Sanguillen.

Such players—from Puerto Rico, Cuba, the Dominican Republic, and more—shared a common language, culture, and customs. Hanging out with them when they came to town surely must have reminded Roberto of his younger days in Carolina, when family and friends made the Clemente house a lively gathering place. These may not have been his **biological** brothers or cousins, but they were like an extended family.

Beyond that, though, Roberto knew he could help out his fellow players from Latin America just by listening and talking with them. He had been there first. He knew the hurdles they faced. That kind of sensitivity to other people's needs and a willingness to help out are what defined Roberto's life off the baseball field.

"Anytime you have an opportunity to make a difference in this world and you don't do it, you are wasting your time on this earth," Roberto once said.

You don't have to be a baseball superstar, of course, to better the world around you. But Roberto's status offered him a platform from which to take advantage of such opportunity.

One way Roberto dreamed of helping out was by building a *Ciudad Deportiva*, or "Sports City," in Carolina. Roberto envisioned Sports City as a place for kids to play sports and learn valuable life lessons. He always liked working with youngsters best. In fact, in most photos of Roberto on the baseball field, he is completely serious. He has his "game face" on. But when working with kids at camps, or teaching a child how to hold a baseball bat or lead off a base, he's beaming.

Wherever Roberto went, helping kids was a priority. That might mean baseball clinics in Puerto Rico or hospital visits in National League cities. Like most baseball stars, Roberto got a lot of fan mail. He would go through the mail himself. Many of the letters had baseball cards or photographs that fans sent him. He'd autograph them and send them back. But

many others were notes from hospitals or sick children. Roberto would sort the notes and letters according to the National League cities from which they came. When the Pirates went on a road trip, he had a stack for each city— say, one for Milwaukee, one for Cincinnati, and one for Chicago on a nine-game trip through the Midwest. Instead of sending the autographs back in the mail, Roberto hand-delivered them directly to the children in the hospitals where they were staying.

Roberto clearly enjoyed such visits. It wasn't only kids that he helped, though. His wife, Vera, once told a reporter that Roberto would rather be late for a meeting with the governor than pass by a stranger who needed help with a tire.

In Roberto's home in Río Piedras, Puerto Rico, people were in and out of the house all the time. They wanted Roberto to speak at the Rotary Club, or they needed help with a charity. The demands were endless. Roberto

could never say no to people in need. He wanted to make a difference.

Roberto made a big difference on the field, too. Even though he turned thirty-six years old—which is not young for a baseball player—in the 1970 season, he had one of his best seasons. He had a .352 batting average, which was the second-best average in his career. The Pirates made the playoffs, but lost before they got to the World Series.

The next season was even better. Roberto hit .341 to rank fourth among all National League batters. The Pirates made the playoffs again, and this time they went to the World Series against the Baltimore Orioles.

The Orioles had a powerful team in 1971. Almost everyone outside of Pittsburgh figured they would beat the Pirates. And sure enough, the Orioles jumped to a big lead in the Series with victories in Games 1 and 2 at Baltimore's Memorial Stadium. Some of the younger Pirates thought it would be hard to turn things around. To win the World Series, a team has to win

The mighty Baltimore Orioles took the lead in the 1971 World Series when they beat the Pirates in each of the first two games.

four games. Since Pittsburgh lost the first two games, to win the series they still had to win four out of the next five games, while Baltimore only needed two more wins. "Don't worry," Roberto told his team. "I will carry the club the rest of the way."

Indeed, the 1971 World Series was Roberto's turn to shine in the national spotlight and show everyone just how good a player he was.

In the third game, the Pirates were clinging to a 2–1 lead in the bottom of the seventh inning. Roberto came to bat against pitcher Mike Cuellar to start off the inning.

Roberto rolled his shoulders, just like he always did. He stretched his back, just like he always did. He held his big bat up high and took a big swing, just like he always did—only this time, he dribbled the ball barely halfway back to the mound.

Mike pounced on the ball quickly and turned to throw to first base. Against most players, it would have been a routine toss for a routine out. But Roberto Clemente never was like most players. When Mike turned, he saw the thirty-seven-year-old Roberto sprinting all out to first base. Startled, Mike hurried his throw, making first baseman John "Boog" Powell step off the bag to make the catch. Roberto was safe at first!

Not long after, Roberto came around to score on Bob Robertson's three-run home run. The Pirates went on to win the game (5–1). Roberto's at-bat in the third game was a key moment of the 1971 World Series. It was hardly his only big play of the Series, though. He also made plays with his bat, arm, and glove, and was named the Series Most Valuable Player. No Latino player before Roberto earned World Series MVP honors.

"I knew he was good," said Brooks Robinson, the Orioles' star third baseman. "But I didn't know he was this good."

In the fourth inning of the decisive Game 7, Roberto came to bat against Mike Cuellar again. Roberto launched a home run over the left center-field wall. Pittsburgh had the lead, and would not give it up. The Pirates won the game

2–1, winning the Series, four games to three. They were World Series champs again.

For the Series, Roberto hit safely in all seven games and batted .414. To this day, Roberto's effort is one of those that baseball fans always remember among the greatest World Series performances ever.

After the final game, reporters crowded around Roberto in the locker room. They thrust microphones in his face and began shouting questions.

"Before I say anything else, I would like to say something for my mother and father in Spanish," Roberto said in English. Then, in his native language, he said: "On the biggest day of my life, I offer blessings to my sons and ask for my parents' blessings in Puerto Rico."

Four days later, Roberto returned to a hero's welcome in Puerto Rico. The governor declared the day a holiday for government employees, and Roberto was surrounded by well-wishers at the airport. Then he was off to the governor's palace. There, he was given a plaque and a gold medal to commemorate his World Series performance.

CHAPTER SEVEN

Tragedy

In a game against the New York Mets in 1972, Roberto notched the 3,000th hit of his Major League career.

The 3,000-hit mark is one of those magical numbers in baseball, like a .300 batting average, or twenty wins in a season, or five hundred home runs in a career. Only ten players reached that mark before Roberto. Only seventeen more have done it since.

The milestone was a major goal for him. As

usual, though, he spoke of the accomplishment in terms of what it meant to others. "I would like to get that many [hits] because it would mean a lot to Latin American people," he said. "My people didn't have a chance to get it before."

On September 30, 1972, Roberto led off the bottom of the fourth inning against Mets left-hander Jon Matlack. Roberto posted his 3,000th hit on a line drive to left-center field. He pulled up into second base on a double and tipped his cap to the crowd. The dignity of the pose has been captured in one of the most famous photographs of his career.

No one knew it at the time, of course, but Roberto's double against Matlack came in the final regular-season at-bat of his career. There were still a few days left on the schedule, but the Pirates wanted the thirty-eight-year-old Roberto to be fresh for the playoffs. Roberto is the only player ever to finish his career with exactly 3,000 hits.

After the Pirates were eliminated by the Cincinnati Reds in the playoffs, Roberto returned to Río Piedras. Then, early in the morning of December 23, a massive earthquake struck Nicaragua. The magnitude 6.2 quake devastated the country. Eighty percent of Nicaragua was leveled. Five thousand people died. More than a quarter of a million people were left without

homes. People were in great need of water, food, and shelter.

Roberto felt a personal connection to the tragedy. He had just been to Managua, Nicaragua, to coach in the Amateur World Series a month earlier. He had walked the streets and talked to the people. He encouraged youngsters and handed out money to people who needed it. As always, if someone was in need and Roberto was in a position to help, he would.

So when Puerto Rican officials asked Roberto to head a local relief effort, of course he said yes. Typically, though, he didn't just lend his name to the charity. He worked. On Christmas Eve and Christmas Day, he loaded supplies. But when word came to him that the supplies were not reaching the people in need, he decided he would accompany the next load himself.

On December 31, 1972—New Year's Eve—Roberto boarded the DC-7 airplane he had

arranged to take from the airport in San Juan to deliver relief supplies for victims of the earthquake.

That load never reached Nicaragua. The plane, which had previous mechanical problems, was overloaded. Barely after takeoff, the pilot tried to turn back. But it was too late. The plane crashed into the ocean. Roberto, the pilot, and three others on board were killed. Roberto's body was never found.

Roberto's tragic death came just three months after his milestone achievement on the baseball field. News of the crash was devastating to family and friends, of course, but also to the baseball world and to all of Puerto Rico. Roberto had touched so many lives around the globe.

In Puerto Rico, Governor-elect Rafael Hernández Colón canceled his inauguration ball and declared three days of national mourning. In the United States, President Richard

Nixon issued a statement: "The best memorial we can build to his memory is to contribute generously to the relief of those he was trying to help." Nixon personally wrote a $1,000 check (worth about $5,500 today) to begin the Roberto Clemente Memorial Fund to help the earthquake victims in Nicaragua.

"We have lost not only a great baseball player, but a wonderful human being," Pirates general manager Joe Brown said. Brown had

been scheduled to fly to Puerto Rico shortly after the first of the year to sign Roberto for his nineteenth season with the Pirates. Roberto had no plans to retire. Though he turned thirty-eight in August 1972, he batted .312 and was an All-Star. He earned his twelfth Gold Glove award. Plus, he was still in marvelous physical shape.

Just four days after Roberto's death, the Baseball Writers' Association of America (BBWAA) requested that the National Baseball Hall of Fame hold a special election for Roberto. The normal waiting period after a player's final game and before he can be inducted into the Hall of Fame is five years. This was only the second time the BBWAA made such a request. The first time was for Lou Gehrig, who died in 1939 of the disease that now bears his name.

Roberto received the necessary votes in the special election. On August 6, 1973, Roberto Clemente Walker became the first Latino player to be inducted into the National Baseball Hall of Fame.

Hall of Fame Plaque

Roberto Clemente's induction into the National Baseball Hall of Fame on August 6, 1973, was a proud day for Latin Americans. There was one mistake, however. His induction plaque read "Roberto Walker Clemente" instead of "Roberto Clemente Walker."

We learned earlier that the custom in Puerto Rico is that the mother's maiden name follows the family name. That's not only a legal distinction, but also an important way to honor the mother's side of the family. The plaque was corrected in 2000.

CHAPTER EIGHT

Legacy

Today, in Pittsburgh, visitors walk across the Roberto Clemente Bridge on the way to PNC Park, where the Pirates play. Outside the park, they see a statue of Roberto. Inside the park, they look out at the Clemente Wall in right field. (The wall is twenty-one feet high, and Roberto's uniform number was 21.) In the Lawrenceville section of the city, visitors gaze at photographs and other memorabilia at the Roberto Clemente Museum.

In San Juan, Puerto Rico, sporting events and concerts are held at the Roberto Clemente Coliseum. That's not far from the Roberto Clemente Sports City in Carolina.

In the Bronx, New York, patients receive care at the Roberto Clemente Center. In Illinois, Maryland, Michigan, New Jersey, Pennsylvania, and other states, students learn at Roberto Clemente schools. Even in faraway Mannheim, Germany, baseball is played at Roberto Clemente Field.

In fact, all over the world, parks, museums, and schools are named after Roberto Clemente.

The students in those schools are the same kids who go to the ballpark and watch players such as Puerto Rico's Carlos Beltran, Venezuela's Carlos Gonzalez, and the Dominican Republic's Albert Pujols star in the Major Leagues. It is a tribute to Roberto that it is no longer unique or noteworthy that they hail from Latin American countries.

In the late 1940s, Philadelphia Athletics catcher Mike Guerra, who was born in Cuba, was the only Latino playing regularly in the big leagues. In 1965, by which time Roberto had become one of baseball's best players, there were forty-eight Latino players. Today, more

than one in every four Major League players was born in Latin America.

It follows that the more Latino players there are in the big leagues, the more they are among those honored in the National Baseball Hall of Fame. After his death, Roberto was the first Latino to be inducted, in 1973. Since then, nine more Latin American–born players have joined Roberto in the Hall of Fame, including Puerto Rico's Orlando Cepeda (inducted in 1999) and Roberto Alomar (inducted in 2011).

New Year's Eve 2012 marked the fortieth anniversary of Roberto's death. Today, he is remembered for his unique batting style, the sliding catches he made in the outfield, his charity work, and his compassion for others. And forty years from now, you can be sure that Roberto will still be remembered for the lasting and positive difference he made on the world.

10 Things

You Should Know
About Roberto Clemente

1 Roberto was born in the town of Carolina, Puerto Rico, on August 18, 1934.

2 He grew up playing baseball with rolled-up rags as a ball and an old broomstick or tree branch as a bat.

3

Roberto's mom wanted him to become an engineer, but he dreamed of becoming a professional ballplayer like the ones he saw play in the Puerto Rican Winter League.

4

He was just eighteen years old when he first started playing professional baseball in Puerto Rico. At nineteen, he signed a contract with Major League Baseball's Brooklyn Dodgers organization.

5 Roberto played in his first Major League game with the Pittsburgh Pirates at age twenty in 1955.

6 The 1961 season was a big year for Roberto. He won the batting title as the player with the best average in the league for the first time. He also won the Gold Glove Award as one of the National League's best defensive players in the outfield for the first of twelve years in a row.

7 Roberto married Vera Zabala in 1964. The couple had three sons: Roberto Jr., Luis, and Enrique.

8 Roberto got his 3,000th hit in 1972 in what turned out to be the last regular-season at-bat of his career.

9 He died in a plane crash on New Year's Eve in 1972 while trying to deliver relief supplies to victims of an earthquake in Nicaragua.

10 The normal five-year waiting period for induction into the National Baseball Hall of Fame was **waived** for Roberto. He was inducted posthumously in 1973.

10 MORE Things

That Are Pretty Cool to Know

1   Roberto's birthplace of Carolina, Puerto Rico, is nicknamed *Tierra de Gigantes*, which means "Land of the Giants."

2   Every year, Major League Baseball presents the Roberto Clemente Award to the player who "demonstrates the values Clemente displayed in his commitment to community and understanding the value of helping others."

3 Roberto helped the Pirates win the World Series twice in his career (1960 and 1971).

4 No Pirates player has worn uniform No. 21 since Roberto did.

5 The Pirates played in Three Rivers Stadium during Roberto's final three seasons (1970–72). Three Rivers Stadium was named because it was built near where the Allegheny River and the Monongahela River **converge** to form the Ohio River.

6 Two of Roberto's sons, Roberto Jr. and Luis, also played professional baseball. But both players had their careers ended by injuries in the minor leagues.

7 The National Baseball Hall of Fame and Museum in Cooperstown, New York, has a permanent display called "Character and Courage." It features life-size statues of all-time greats Roberto Clemente, Lou Gehrig, and Jackie Robinson.

8 When Roberto was inducted into the National Baseball Hall of Fame in 1973, another player who was inducted that year was Monte Irvin— the professional player who befriended Roberto when Roberto was a youngster.

9 The Pirates now play their home games at PNC Park in Pittsburgh. The right–field wall there is twenty–one feet high, in honor of Roberto's uniform number.

10 To many fans of the Pittsburgh Pirates, Roberto still is known simply as "the Great One."

Glossary

Barrio: a part of a city or town in a Spanish-speaking country

Biological: direct relatives

Converge: come together

Debut: first appearance

Discrimination: prejudice or unjust behavior to others based on age, race, gender, etc.

Guava: a tropical fruit that is yellowish in color, and round or pear-shaped

Injustice: something unfair

Innovation: a new idea or invention

Machetes: large knives with heavy blades

Makeshift: something that works as a substitute for the real thing

Migrate: to change location with a change in seasons

Posthumously: occurring after death

Rapport: a harmonious relationship

Rookie: a first-year participant in an organized sport or activity

Rural: a country setting

Segregation: the separation of a race, class, or ethnic group

Unique: one of a kind

Waived: set aside or put off

Places to Visit

Are you interested in learning more about Roberto Clemente and baseball history? Whether you visit online or in real life, here are some places that will help you cover all the bases!

National Baseball Hall of Fame and Museum, Cooperstown, New York
The official site of baseball's Hall of Fame is a trove of baseball history.
baseballhall.org

PNC Park, Pittsburgh, Pennsylvania
The current home of the Pittsburgh Pirates.
pittsburgh.pirates.mlb.com/pit/ballpark/ index.jsp

The Clemente Museum, Pittsburgh, Pennsylvania

Home to the largest collection of memorabilia dedicated solely to Roberto Clemente.

clementemuseum.com

Bibliography

¡Beisbol!: Latino Baseball Pioneers and Legends, Jonah Winter, Lee & Low Books, 2001.

Clemente!, Willie Perdomo, Illustrated by Bryan Collier, Henry Holt and Company, 2010.

Roberto Clemente (Baseball Hall of Famers), Robert Kingsbury, Rosen Publishing Group, 2003.

Roberto Clemente (Baseball Legends), Peter C. Bjarkman, Chelsea House Publications, 1991.

Roberto Clemente (Hispanics of Achievement), Thomas W. Gilbert, Chelsea House Publications, 1991.

Roberto Clemente: Pride of the Pittsburgh Pirates, Jonah Winter, Illustrated by Raúl Colón, Atheneum Books for Young Readers, 2005.

Index

Also Available

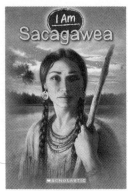

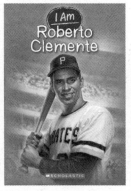